Res Burman's Poetry
Volume 2

RES J F BURMAN

Writers' Champion

Res Burman's Poetry Volume 2

The right of Res J. F Burman to be identified as the author of this work has been asserted in accordance with sections 77 and 78 of the Copyright Design and Patent Act 1988.

Copyright © Res J. F Burman 2022
For information contact via email: res.burman@outlook.com

All text materials taken from Res's on line blog: http://resswritingandpoetry.blogspot.co.uk

Published through Writers' Champion imprint of MAPublisher (Penzance)
www.mapublisher.org.uk, email: mapublisher@yahoo.com
Printed in UK via Print on Demand

ISBN-13: 978-1-910499-93-1

All rights reserved. No part of this publication may be reproduced, stored in a retrieval system, or transmitted, in any form or by any means, electronic, mechanical, photocopying, recording, public performances or otherwise, without prior written permission of the copyright holder, except for brief quotations embodied in critical articles or reviews.

Disclaimer:
All expressions and opinions of the work belong to the artists/writer, and WC does not share or endorse any other than to provide the open platform to publish their work. For further information on WC policies please email: above email for further information and for submission guidelines.

Book layout, typesetting and cover designed by Mayar Akash
Cover image by Res Burman
Typeset in Times Roman

Paper printed on is FSC Certified, lead free, acid free, buffered paper made from wood-based pulp. Our paper meets the ISO 9706 standard for permanent paper. As such, paper will last several hundred years when stored.

Res J. F. Burman

Dedication

This book is dedicated to my son Ruan, who after 44 years is still the best thing that ever happened to me.

Acknowledgements

I would like to thank my Publisher Mayar Akash of MAPublisher (Penzance) for his hard work and encouragement in getting these books to press.

I'd also like to thank all those who have read my work and encouraged me over the years, especially those who have now gone before us.

Without our readers we poets would be but dust in the wind.
Thank you.

Contents

Dedication	3
Acknowledgements	4
Introductions.	13
Interesting Times	18
November Eyes a haiku	19
Transatlantic Flight a tanka	19
Maiden's Blush a haiku	19
Morning's Light a tanka	19
Storm Clouds a haiku	20
Funeral	20
Wet Today	20
Are You There	20
Mist a gogyoshi	21
Acceptance a haiku	21
Remembered	21
Waves	21
Blue a haiku	21
Fever	22
Glory a haiku	22
Dawn Confirms a haiku	22
Treasure a haiku	22
A-sailing a haiku	23
Fishermen a haiku	23
Magic Moment a haiku	23
Godolphin Hill a haiku	23
Goddess Grant a haiku	23
The Dawn	24
Every Cloud a haiku	24
Better Days Coming a haiku	24
Peckish a haiku	24
Life's Longing for Itself a haiku	24
Oyster a haiku	25
Cornwall My Home a haiku	25
Hope on the Skyline a haiku	25
The Old King a haiku	25
God's Canvas a tanka	25
Glowering Clouds a gogyoshi	26
Cold Still Clings a haiku	26
Monochrome a tanka	26
Peace a tanka	26
The Huffpost a gogyoshi	27

Police Violence a gogyoshi	27
Lonesome Cry a haiku	27
Polished a haiku	27
Glowering Clouds a haiku	28
The Bird a haiku	28
Showers a haiku	28
Warmth a haiku	28
Heaven a haiku	28
A Quiet Moment a haiku	29
Before Dawn a haiku	29
Women's Day a haiku	29
Breakfast a haiku	29
Blood Red Dawn a haiku	29
Sunlight a haiku	30
Excited Insects a haiku	30
St Piran's Day a haiku	30
Gloomy Weather a haiku	30
Other Worlds a haiku	30
Mist a tanka	31
Rays a tanka	31
Rudi a gogyoshi	31
Solitary Flight a haiku	31
Seagull a haiku	31
Your Smile. An Ode to my Post Lady	32
Angel's Wing a gogyoshi	32
Morning Sunshine a haiku	33
Hope a haiku	33
Sand a tanka	33
Dancing in the Dark a gogyoshi	33
Oh the Sunshine a haiku	33
Monterey Pine a gogyoshi	34
The Holy Headland a tanka	34
Sound of the Waves a haiku	34
The Telephone Box a tanka	34
Mongolia a gogyoshi	35
Two Gulls a haiku	35
The Mount and the Dragon a haiku	35
The Tennessee Waltz a tanka	35
Ash Wednesday a haiku	35
Dragon's Resting a haiku	36
St Valentine's Day a gogyoshi	36
Storms and Rain haiku	36
Unforgiving Seas a haiku	36

Sunbeams a haiku	36
My Last Will and Testament a tanka	37
Revenge a haiku	37
Shiver me Timbers a haiku	37
February Blues a haiku	37
Fifty Shades a haiku	37
Echoing Footsteps a haiku	38
The Mount and the Dragon a gogyoshi	38
The Pilgrim a tanka	38
Flights of Fancy haiku	38
Guiding Light haiku	39
Hunger Games haiku	39
Stone Lantern a gogyoshi	39
Roofs gogyoshi	39
The Blues haiku	39
Rise of Spring haiku	40
The Mount haiku	40
Bounty of the Seas gogyoshi	40
No View haiku	40
Mist and Rain haiku	40
Covid jab haiku	41
Dragon in the mist haiku	41
Chimneys of Battlefields haiku	41
Fog haiku	41
Seagulls haiku	41
Denver Scanesa gogyoshi	42
Pastel Promises haiku	42
Cold Sea haiku	42
Winter Requirements haiku	42
Shuttered Doors haiku	42
Lockdown Isolation haiku	43
Dragon Sleeps haiku	43
Pale Sun haiku	43
The Blues haiku	43
Steam haiku	43
Patch of Blue tanka	44
Morning Cold haiku	44
North East Wind haiku	44
Hope haiku	44
Calm haiku	44
Wet Morning haiku	45
Autumn Equinox haiku	45
De Gallant haiku	45

Blackwing haiku	45
Poppy haiku	45
Coronavirus	46
Pastel Morning haiku	46
Miss England tanka	46
Silver Sea haiku	46
Ann's Gardens	47
Coloured Lights haiku	48
Coughing tanka	48
Polished haiku	48
Two Metre Separation haiku	48
If I Go Away haiku	48
Today a Pigeon haiku	49
Ready for the fray haiku	49
Setsubun haiku	49
The Sentry haiku	49
When We Were Young	49
Friday 13th December 2019	50
Sunlit Castle haiku	51
Dusk haiku	51
Aerial Aviator haiku	51
Cornish November haiku	51
Morning Visitor haiku	51
It's That Sort of Day haiku	52
Chinese Seasons Frost Descends haiku	52
The Penzance Lineman gogyoshi	52
Summer Sunshine tanka	52
Mountain Airs haiku	52
The Pub Cat haiku	53
Norfolk Island Pine II haiku	53
Night Cramps	53
Today I'm Blue!	55
Door Stepping a haiku chain	56
Rainy Day haiku	56
Love's Ambassadors haiku	57
Sea Fever haiku	57
The Carrion Crow haiku	57
Heaven's Messenger haiku	57
A Jackdaw haiku	57
Night Mist haiku	58
Godolphin Hill haiku	58
May Dawn haiku	58
Forever Young a tanka	58

A Hungry Jackdaw haiku	58
The Year of the Ox a tanka	59
Dreaming II a tanka	59
Dreaming tanka	59
Eagle Screams a haiku	59
Primroses haiku	60
Mercy tanka	60
Bosoms and Halter Tops haiku	60
Panama Hat haiku	60
Evening G & T haiku	60
I Wish I Were....	61
Valentine's Day haiku	62
Kuching haiku	62
Keep Your Hammer Face Polished	62
November Mornings haiku	63
The Great West Road	64
Haiku Road	65
Green for Gold haiku	65
Morning Sun haiku	65
A Divine Hand haiku	66
Waning Days haiku	66
The Conservative Party Conference haiku	66
Sparkling Waters haiku	66
Fools Knocking haiku	66
Michelle	67
Away with the Birds haiku	67
Bowing haiku	67
Trishaw Man haiku	68
The Garlic Revolution gogyoshi	68
Autumn Airs gogyoshi	68
Come Away!	68
Denver Scanes gogyoshi	69
Skirmishing with The Little 'C'	70
Rain tanka	71
Politics two haiku	71
Collared Doves haiku	72
Seeking the Shadows haiku	72
Precious Moment haiku	72
Gentle Rain haiku	72
Saint Crispin's Day haiku	72
John Steinbeck's Pencil haiku	73
Scribbler's Delight haiku	73
Bad Planning	73

Evening Musings haiku and tanka	74
Foxgloves Await haiku	74
Buddha's Care haiku	74
TickaTacka haiku	75
Headache haiku	75
Foxgloves haiku	75
Bamboo haiku	75
True Friendship	75
Alsatian Puppy haiku	76
Paddy haiku	76
Young Once haiku	76
Hindu Jewel haiku	76
Autumn Glory haiku	76
Autumn Airs	77
Red Mugs	77
The East is Always Calling tanka	77
845 NACS haiku	78
Going to Market haiku	78
Alms haiku	78
Tall Bamboo haiku	78
Jungle Patrol haiku	79
Eagles haiku	79
The Earth Pin	79
Pneumonia a tanka	80
Greek Steps haiku	80
Basho's Grave haiku	80
Jungle haiku chain	81
Yorkshire Tea haiku	81
Red Threads tanka	81
Kisses	82
Hero Monks haiku	82
Seagull haiku	82
Shy Smile haiku	82
Bonzo& Lobo haiku	83
Bonzo haiku	83
Longan Harvest haiku	83
Oh Barcelona haiku	83
Fire haiku	83
Holstered Pistol haiku	84
Robin Williams haiku	84
Tweeting haiku	84
Bamboos droop haiku	84
Lavender Lady haiku	84

Brompton Road haiku chain	85
Tidying Up	86
Pine Straw	90
Strawberries and Cream	91
No One	92
Zhang Ziyi haiku	92
This Country In Between	93
Singapore Customs	93
The Death of a Hooray Henry	95
Misty Dreams	96
The Old Cormorant Fisherman	96
Hanging Bookshelf	97
Rest in Peace, Robin Williams	97
Why Do We Bother To Remember The Dead?	97
Qǐngchīmǐfàn	98
Fanning the Flames (For Niall O'Connor)	99
Another Young Friend Lost	99
Another Young Friend Lost	100
Shopkeeper	101
Spring haiku	101
The Wicked Witch	101
Index	103
MAPublisher Catalogue	110

Introductions.

"We've salt in our veins
And there's tar on our hands
Let's once more away
And seek foreign lands.

And if I find I'm too old
Or I do not have the means
I will still sail the oceans
On a ship of my dreams!"

On Facebook, I used to go by the alias of Driftwood, definitely I could always relate to the ship of the dreams of my friend for over a decade, Res Burman. Connecting over this social media and virtual space, I have always felt a soul connect with Res. We share many common interests some of them undefinable like being seasoned fellow veterans of different Armies, having seen action in different eras and geographical regions, a bond deeper than East meets West.

"I've danced with Death a time or two
And so far come off best
But there's no kind of certainty
That I'll always pass the test.

I've skirmished with the best of 'em
Picked up a scar or two
Had a close encounter with a bayonet
But it didn't run me through."

We may not have bled together, but there is a deep understanding that no matter the varying motifs or colours on our flags, we bleed the same crimson colour.

Poems of Res are like a breath of fresh air, unpretentious and lucid. The wise old man has imbibed an immense wealth of Eastern philosophy and blended it dexterously with his rational western approach.

Res is uninhibited when his poems explore nature and seasons.

"God's Canvas" a tanka
"The view this morning
Was misty and grey... as though
It was God's canvas

Waiting for the Holy Hand
To paint Her Glory upon it"

Res experiments boldly with Haiku and tanka, and is able to deliver the essence of each of these styles. Another recurring theme in many of his poems are nature and seasons and how they affect the fragility of humans

"Autumn airs bring a chill
To my old bones
And my left foot
Which has no feeling
Or big toe nail.... aches!"

The overwhelming sense of aloneness, of loss, finds voice in poems of Res, not as a scream or whimper but simply as a stated fact.

" Someone gave us silver
And took all our colour
In exchange"

Res has been a military veteran and has an inimitable bonding with dogs. We share this mutual love and respect for dogs as man's best friend.

"Lantern hanging in the trees,
Full moon overhead,
An orange moon, a bloody moon,
As I buried my dead!

She'd been a lover for many a year,
A friend so true and brave,
But under that bloody moon
I slaved to dig her grave.
Lantern hanging in the trees,

Full moon looks down scowling
An orange moon, a bloody moon,
I swear I heard it howling!"

I placed some stones above her,
And marked it with a log,
And whispered to her, as oft before,
"Lobo. Stay. Good Dog! "

There is so much more to read, absorb and relish in the poems of Old Soldier, Traveller, Herdsman, Cow-lifter, Builder, Forester, Carpenter, Cabinetmaker, Woodturner, War Pensioner, Father, Taoist, Photographer, Poet, Lover, Res Burman.

Happy reading, folks.

Lt Colonel Shyam Sunder Sharma, Shaurya Chakra (Retired)
India, War Wounded & Decorated Veteran, Poet, Birdwatcher and Nature lover.

You're holding in your hands a collection of the poems of Res J.F. Burman, an old soldier, a world traveller, a Taoist, a father, a photographer, a woodturner, and a man known by many as the Pirate of Penzance. Res is a man who is beloved by many readers in far-flung places, one who has outlived his contemporaries and now faces the loneliness of life's later years with courage and grace.

Res writes of what he knows. Whether commenting on his war experiences, his luck and blessings in love, his encounters with Leonard Cohen in London, his time in Matala in Greece where a young Joni Mitchell found inspiration leading to her masterful Blue album, Res reveals the gentle mastery of a man who has seen a lot and written of it humbly, with heart and wisdom. And when he speaks of his pain and fury, addressing challenges and injustices, Res does so with authority.

Where Res lives in Penzance he has a unique and steadfast view of the world, of the sea and the changing skies. He celebrates the glories and mercies of his days through writing and photography, sharing them across the globe with people who've come to know and love his work. This book is a testament to his goodness and talents, a book that marks a victory of the human kind, a survival of storms, a man's ongoing search for meaning, for what truly matters in life.

Doug Lang
Vancouver, Canada
Musician, Prairie Poet and Radio DJ at "Better Days" and "Riverside Drive" on Vancouver Co-op Radio.

Res is a national treasure and this spills forth in his poetry telling of life, love, bygone times and of his many adventures.

His strong compassion for his fellow man shines throughout and it is obvious that Res is a man with much heart. I'm sure yours will be touched many times while reading his poems..

He has a knack for that and also for bringing alive stories of old with emotions and images vividly painted in all their diversity.

I feel blessed to know Res and privileged to have gained a glimpse into his extraordinary life told through his poetry.

I'm sure you will too.

Tina Purplenblue Clowes Kay.
Hill Walker, Poet and Photographer Extraordinaire.

~~~~~~

Res Burman's poetry is like a cool wind, the softest ocean in the summer & a bright blue sky filled with the echo of singing birds. His words surround you like a playful & passionate lover who swims inside your heart and mind. His biggest fan,

Gina Nemo
Gina Nemo is an American actress, singer, author, poet and marketing executive who had an award-winning role as Dorothy Pezzino in the American television series 21 Jump Street in the 1980s. She runs her own Film Actors School. She is the daughter of jazz musician Henry Nemo.

Res Burman. A Londoner, a seasoned soldier, who long ago left the rat race behind for a quite life in Cornwall. I have got to know him through his writing and discovered a man of wisdom and wit! Put in simple terms, Res comes to life on the page. An old pirate now, he brings Cornwall to the page for everyone to read, to delight in, his words, sometimes accompanied by photographs, always giving us a close up view of what he calls Pirate Central! A man of charm and compassion, he has a way of bringing the natural world and the human world together like no other poet. His love for the wild animals and wild places come together on the pagein perfect harmony. Crafted to perfection, his poetry is simple, sometimes outrageous, serious, humorous and always so readable.

Affection for his natural surroundings, love of his fellow man, a craving for justice and fairness for all, Res Burman is, in my opinion, a go to poet. A man for all occasions. And as I sit here writing this now, I can imagine Res sat at his desk in the window, pen in hand looking out over the rooftops to the sea, the tide sweeping new words over the shoreline of his mind. A wise man, a funny man, a friend, a writer without equal. So, pull up a chair, make yourself comfortable, and lose yourself in the words of this Fine poet. Believe me, you will be glad you did.

Dennis Moriarty
Another Londoner who escaped the rat race for Rural South Wales, Master Poet,

Interesting Times

Our warm spell is over
And though it is Easter
"Heat or Eat" has become
The motto of millions!

"Warm the Human not the home"
Is the new catchphrase
As millions huddle under blankets
And sleeping bags just to stay warm.

This Energy Poverty takes its toll
On the poor and the sick
And the elderly
No matter who they voted for

We find we cannot eat the lies
That our Government feeds us
We cannot warm our homes or ourselves
On the broken promises that burn before us

And we're told it will only get worse
And perhaps we deserve no better
When we allow the tyrants to prosper
And the dishonest to rule.

This is the cross we Britons must bear
Because we allowed those who should protect us
To fill their pockets instead
To guzzle at the trough of their own greed.

We have allowed Newspaper magnates
To do our thinking for us
And form our opinions and prejudices
Are we just puppets on strings?

We have lost control of our country
And our disinterest and inaction
Brings the old Chinese curse closer
"May you live in interesting times!"

31st March 2022

November Eyes a haiku

November eyes drawn
Beyond the Chip Shop chimney
To where dreams are born

4th November 2021

Transatlantic Flight a tanka

Transatlantic flight
Too high to be seen or heard
But she leaves a clue

Painted across the heavens
As she speeds towards the dawn

22nd October 2021

Maiden's Blush a haiku

Storm clouds blow away
Revealing a maiden's blush
On our horizon

22 October 2021

Morning's Light a tanka

Morning's early light
Ignores the sleeping Dragon
But shines down upon

The Lizard's windmills
And Goonhilly's listening ears

22nd October 2021

Storm Clouds a haiku

Storm clouds gather
The sea takes on strange colours
Winter creeps closer

21st October 2021

Funeral

The Church bell behind the chimney
Tolls
Pealing far and wide
Another Brother or Sister gone
The chimneys sit silently
Watching the souls of the dead arise

19th October 2021

Wet Today

The clocks say
Morning has broken
But my eyes deny it
More like zero dark thirty
And the post lady's boots
Are going to be wet today

18th October 2021

Are You There

The blue horizon
Calls me yonder
Beneath one single streak
Of fire.... above my head
It makes me wonder
Are you still out there?

17th October 2021

Mist a gogyoshi

The mist kisses the windows
And the sun is but a rumour
Or a secret told shyly
From wet roof to wet rooftop
And chimney to chimney pot

14th October 2021

Acceptance a haiku

We take the weather
As she comes... we have no say
Acceptance is all

9th June 2021

Remembered

There may yet come a day
When good men are remembered
Not for daring deeds or mighty works
But for what they left behind
Maybe for the hearts they touched
Or perhaps for the trees they planted

1st June 2021

Waves

The rain will wet us
And the wind will blow today
Waves to wash our sins away

20th May 2021

Blue a haiku

It's a blue blue day
Enough cloud to cast shadows
On the shiny sea

13th May 2021

Fever

The unforgiving eye of insomnia and delirium
Skittering among the dark trees of the bedroom ceiling
The cracks in the plaster portals to another more horrifying world
Eight days waiting for the correct medicine to reduce my fever
And fight this infection

While the Black Dog prowls among the dark trees... and howls
And in my stupor I cannot be certain if the howls are his or mine.
And the question most often asked is
Is this the way old soldiers are sent home to die?
Without even a Goodbye Kiss
Is this the way old soldiers are sent home to die?

24th April 2021

Glory a haiku

Night gives way to day
Slowly and reluctantly
A Blaze of Glory

18th April 2021

Dawn Confirms a haiku

The Dawn confirms
Cancer and Covid free
So far So good

17th April 2021

Treasure a haiku

Silver enough
To fill my pockets
Pirate treasure

15th April 2021

Res J. F. Burman

A-sailing a haiku

Is there enough blue
To sew me a Sailor's Suit
I must go a-sailing

14th April 2021

Fishermen a haiku

Low low clouds today
Between the sea and the sky
Fishermen endure

31st March 2021

Magic Moment a haiku

That magic moment
When all is still and waiting
For what day may bring

30th March 2021

Godolphin Hill a haiku

The sun rises
From behind Godolphin Hill
Summer hope takes flight

30th March 2021

Goddess Grant a haiku

Goddess grant that Spring
Come to us with open hands
Her Treasures to share

28th March 2021

The Dawn

To plagiarize my friend
Rudyard Kipling
An' the dawn comes up like thunder
Outer the Lizard 'crost the bay!

27th March 2021

Every Cloud a haiku

Every Cloud
Has its own silver lining
Some sayings come true

26th March 2021

Better Days Coming a haiku

The day starts pretty
As Spring skips gaily closer
Better Days coming

25hth March 2021

Peckish a haiku

'Ere Gert, d'you fancy
A really really big fish
I'm a bit peckish

(Whale sighted in the Bay!)

24th March 2021

Life's Longing for Itself a haiku

Out over the sea
A single gull searches for food
Life's longing for itself

23rd March 2021

Res J. F. Burman

Oyster a haiku

Seagull warms itsfeet
On the Chippy chimney pot
The world's his oyster

23rd March 2021

Cornwall My Home a haiku

So clear this morning
Harry Glasson could see me waving
Singing "Cornwall My Home"

22nd March 2021

Hope on the Skyline a haiku

Between sea and sky
A narrow band of bright light
Hope on the skyline

22nd March 2021

The Old King a haiku

The Old King gazes
Upon his Kingdom... wondering
What the hell happened

21 March 2021

God's Canvas a tanka

The view this morning
Was misty and grey... as though
It was God's canvas

Waiting for the Holy Hand
To paint Her Glory upon it

20th March 2021

25

Glowering Clouds a gogyoshi

These glowering clouds
Sometimes fly so low
It seems we're about to be crushed

Tall men walk with a stoop
And seagulls have to duck their heads

19th March 2021

Cold Still Clings a haiku

The Sun gets stronger
As Spring seems to get closer
But the cold still clings

18th March 2021

Monochrome a tanka

Sometimes the Sun
Jealous of competition
Absorbs all colour

But the chimney pots remain
Monochrome in this bright light

17th March 2021

Peace a tanka

The eternal conflict
Between darkness and light
Is best seen here

Dawn brings equilibrium
The coming of light brings Peace

16th March 2021

The Huffpost a gogyoshi

"Undercover Police Officers could police Nightclubs
to Better Protect Women!"
The Huffpost

The Government says
It'll put Police Officers
In Night Clubs to Protect Women
What springs first to your mind
"Cat among the Pigeons?"

16th March 2021

Police Violence a gogyoshi

It appears to me the Metropolitan Police
Resent the fact that one of their number
A colleague, has been arrested for murder
So they took revenge upon grieving women
Who already felt unsafe upon the streets

15th March 2021

Lonesome Cry a haiku

The dawn creeps closer
Easing its way through the clouds
Seagull's lonesome cry

15th March 2021

Polished a haiku

The sea looks polished
As if by some giant hand
Spring edges closer

14th March 2021

Glowering Clouds a haiku

Low glowering clouds
Shed rain upon the Lizard
Winter's grasping hands

13th March 2021

The Bird a haiku

Even the Gulls are
Giving the weather the bird
Staying close to home

12th March 2021

Showers a haiku

Sunlight is sparkling
On wet slates and chimney pots
Between the showers

11th March 2021

Warmth a haiku

Penzance just sits there
On a cold but sunny day
Praying for more warmth

10th March 2021

Heaven a haiku

As the sun rises
The dawn chorus always starts
Gull's homage to Heaven

9th March 2021

A Quiet Moment a haiku

A quiet moment
When even the gulls are hushed
Waiting for the day

9th March 2021

Before Dawn a haiku

Before dawn the Sun
Paints pastel shades across the sky
The World holds her breath

8th March 2021

Women's Day a haiku

Today's Women's Day
May the Sun shine upon 'em
Bless them... ev'ry one

8th March 2021

Breakfast a haiku

The lone gull takes flight
Looking for her next breakfast
In the blood red dawn

7th March 2021

Blood Red Dawn a haiku

The sun is rising
But the Castle still stands firm
In this blood red dawn

7th March 2021

Sunlight a haiku

Sunlight falls like rain
Through narrow gaps in the clouds
Spotlights on water

6th March 2021

Excited Insects a haiku

The Chinese fortnight
Of the Excited Insects
Lead us towards spring

5th March 2021

St Piran's Day a haiku

Thank God for Cornwall
Now on this Saint Piran's Day
Paradise on earth

5th March 2021

Gloomy Weather a haiku

Even my neighbours
Tire of this gloomy weather
Oh spring... where art thou?

4th March 2021

Other Worlds a haiku

Somewhere in the mist
There are other worlds... hidden
From my searching eyes

3rd March 2021

Mist a tanka

The world vanishes
Behind a veil of pale mist
Is anyone there?

In days of isolation
Even the gulls look for friends

2nd March 2021

Rays a tanka

Early morning rays
Give hope to our feathered friends
It's St David's Day

1st March 2021

Rudi a gogyoshi

My dear friend Rudi
Moved away and left
No forwarding address
I was promised conjugal visits
Dogs keep their promises.... humans don't

27th February 2021

Solitary Flight a haiku

With a mewing cry
Seemingly effortless grace
Solitary flight

27th February 2021

Seagull a haiku

First hint of sunshine
And this chap puts on his best
And goes a-courting

26th February 2021

Your Smile. An Ode to my Post Lady

If I had my way Your smile would be
Declared A National Treasure
Your smile radiates
Kindness and compassion
Good nature and friendship
I'd have it printed
On all the stamps
So Royal Mail could carry
Your image the length and breadth
Of the Country
And Air-mail too
So all the world could see
The beauty of your smile.

I'd have it printed on Banknotes
So perhaps it would make us
More sensible with money
Preferring to keep your image
Close to our hearts
And if darkness enfolds us
As sometimes it will
Your smile will bring light
Into our worlds
And beauty into our hearts
We need more smiles
We all need more smiles
But most of all
We need the beauty of yours!

25th February 2019

Angel's Wing a gogyoshi

Just a hint of pink in the sky
So fleeting, ephemeral
And then it's gone
Quiet as a whisper in your ear
Or a caress from and Angel's Wing

24th February 2021

Morning Sunshine a haiku

Rainbows don't lead us
To a pot of gold... Oh no
It's morning sunshine

26th February 2021

Hope a haiku

Like sailors of old
My eyes seek the horizon
Hope on the skyline

25th February 2021

Sand a tanka

Crash upon crash
The waves thunder on the shore
Driven by the wind

But the gulls have seen it all
Turning granite into sand

23rd February 2021

Dancing in the Dark a gogyoshi

Dancing in the dark
With my lover's arms around me
And her sweet whispers in my ear
These are but dreams of yesteryear
That even age will not decay

22nd February 2021

Oh the Sunshine a haiku

The Mount and the Dragon
Floating upon misty seas
But Oh the sunshine

22nd February 2021

Monterey Pine a gogyoshi

A magnificent Monterey Pine
Generous with its shade and shelter
Watches over the Penzance dead
In a black and white photograph
Like the dead... frozen in time

22nd February 2021

The Holy Headland a tanka

Old Saint Mary's Church
Sits high above the Dry Dock
Penzance Harbour view

Landmark known to all sailors
Pen Sans - The Holy Headland

21st February 2021

Sound of the Waves a haiku

Solitary gull
It's mewing almost drowned out
The sound of the waves

21st February 2021

The Telephone Box a tanka

The telephone box
Forever lost in the woods
Still waiting for THAT call

Long distance information
Get in touch with my Marie

20th February 2021

Mongolia a gogyoshi

Oh Mongolia
Rugged enough to breed strong people
Beautiful enough bring a song
To their loving hearts
And a smile to their lovely faces

20th February 2021.

Two Gulls a haiku

So dull this morning
Today was almost cancelled
Then two gulls came by

19th February 2021

The Mount and the Dragon a haiku

The Mount and the Dragon
Snooze in early morning sun
Calm after the storm

18th February 2021

The Tennessee Waltz a tanka

The Tennessee Waltz
Briefly brings tears to my eyes
Passing like a cloud

A forgotten memory
Plumbing the well of my mind

18th February 2021

Ash Wednesday a haiku

It's a blue morning
This Ash Wednesday... the sixth
Day of the Ash Moon

17th February 2021

Dragon's Resting a haiku

The Dragon's resting
Upon a bed of pale mist
But some still seek food

16th February 2021

St Valentine's Day a gogyoshi

It's February fourteenth
St Valentine's Day
I wonder is my love still out there
Across these wasteful years
And across these angry seas

14th February 2021

Storms and Rain haiku

We have storms and rain
C'mon now... year of the ox
You can do better

13th February 2021

Unforgiving Seas a haiku

Not as rough today
But still rough enough to kill
Unforgiving seas

12th February 2021

Sunbeams a haiku

This morning's sunbeams
Bring some illumination
But none for us here

8th February 2021

Res J. F. Burman

My Last Will and Testament a tanka

Helluva crash bang
My Last Will and Testament
Just fell on my head

It just leapt off the bookcase
Let's hope it's not an omen

12th February 2021

Revenge a haiku

Oh these angry waves
Pound against our granite quays
Searching for revenge

11th February 2021

Shiver me Timbers a haiku

Winter comes storming
With wild winds and crashing waves
Shiver me timbers

11th February 2021

February Blues a haiku

It is that damp cold
That penetrates these old bones
February blues

10th February 2021

Fifty Shades a haiku

Fifty shades of grey
But it's too cold for romance
Gull seeks warm chimney

9th February 2021

Echoing Footsteps a haiku

Echoing footsteps
And the raucous cry of gulls
Speak to us of dawn

8th February 2021

The Mount and the Dragon a gogyoshi

The Mount and the Dragon
Slumber in the misty dawn
As the cold returns
But it's the Northern Spring Equinox on Mars
I wonder if it's warmer there

7th February 2021

The Pilgrim a tanka

It was snowy peaks
And mighty jungle rivers
Led this Pilgrim here

To find tranquillity now
At the feet of the Goddess

7th February 2021

Flights of Fancy haiku

Early morning sun
Lifts the imagination
These flights of fancy

6th February 2021

Guiding Light haiku

On Saint Michael's Mount
There's a light in the window
Guiding sailors home

5th February 2021

Hunger Games haiku

These are Hunger Games
Played out on air and water
Hungry winter months

5th February 2021

Stone Lantern a gogyoshi

Old stone lantern in a Japanese garden
I wonder whose breath last extinguished the flame
Was it sweet and fragrant or sour with age
Did they seek to plunge the garden to darkness
Or merely make ready for the bright light of day

4th February 2021

Roofs gogyoshi

The roofs of old Penzance
Soaking up the first sunshine
Of the year
Growing moss and grass
And sheltering so many dreams

4th February 2021

The Blues haiku

Risshun... Rise of Spring
Creeps across our horizon
Still we sing the blues

4th February 2021

Rise of Spring haiku

In Cornwall's sunrise
Hope is sown in pastel skies
Chinese Rise of Spring

3rd February 2021

The Mount haiku

Winter's early sun
Shines on the roofs of the town
The Mount in the mist

2nd February 2021

Bounty of the Seas gogyoshi

On the doorstep of Saint Michael's Mount
A fishing boat plies it's trade
A beacon for all the hungry gulls
Who also earn their living
From the bounty of the seas

3rd February 2021

No View haiku

There's no view today
These days of torrential rain
Washed the view away

1st February 2021

Mist and Rain haiku

Mist and rain so thick
Even the seagulls are lost
Circling hungry skies

31st January 2021

Res J. F. Burman

Covid jab haiku

The rain it raineth
Yet again ... never-ending
Covid jab today

30th January 2021

Dragon in the mist haiku

Out there in the bay
The dragon sleeps in the mist
She's waiting for spring

29th January 2021

Chimneys of Battlefields haiku

As if to keep warm
The chimneys of Battlefields
Clustered together

28th January 2021

Fog haiku

Today we have fog
So our view is curtailed
And seagulls stay home

27th January 2021

Seagulls haiku

There are those who say
Seagulls are drowned sailor's souls
Today they're screaming

26th January 2021

Denver Scanesa gogyoshi

My old friend Denver
Still looms large in my life
Even in Death
His kind words linger, as does his laughter
In an echo on my telephone wire

25th January 2021

Pastel Promises haiku

Steam from the sea
Rising into the cold air
Pastel promises

25th January 2021

Cold Sea haiku

Good Morning my World
We have some clouds and sunshine
Above our cold sea

23rd January 2021

Winter Requirements haiku

Winter requirements
A good fire and boundless faith
Should carry us through

20th January 2021

Shuttered Doors haiku

Behind shuttered doors
The isolated still pray
Please remember me

20th January 2021

Lockdown Isolation haiku

These grey winter days
Even our view is tear stained
Lockdown isolation

20th January 2021

Dragon Sleeps haiku

The Dragon's sleeping
But her distant relatives
Still soar through the mist

19th January 2021

Pale Sun haiku

A pale sun looks down
Upon the cold misty sea
Oh Spring.... Where art thou?

17th January 2021

The Blues haiku

There's just enough breeze
To lift the wings of a gull
Floating on the blues

16th January 2021

Steam haiku

Steam on the water
Even the morning sunshine
Feels cold on my skin

15th January 2021

Patch of Blue tanka

Today it's cloudy
Cold with a chance of showers
In the Penzance skies

But a gull flies overhead
Looking for that patch of blue

14th January 2021

Morning Cold haiku

Morning cold and still
But the sunshine heralds
Warmer days to come

10th January 2021

North East Wind haiku

This cold north east wind
Chills my bones and stings my ears
My eyes flood with tears

9th January 2021

Hope haiku

Is that hope I see
Upon our far horizon
When we need it most

9th January 2021

Calm haiku

After bad weather
Nature takes out her pastels
Calm over the Bay

17th December 2020

Wet Morning haiku

Over slate grey roofs
And terracotta chimneys
Salt spray reigns supreme

16th December 2020

Autumn Equinox haiku

Autumn Equinox
Comes stealing across the bay
As shy as a maid

22nd September 2020

De Gallant haiku

Dawn crept in shyly
Like a ghost ship under sail
Barely a whisper

11th September 2020

Blackwing haiku

The Blackwing Pencil
Lusting for the spoken word
Ready for duty

7th August 2020

Poppy haiku

Our English Poppy
Bows and blows to every breeze
Remembrance always

24th June 2020

Coronavirus

I presented my urine sample
At my Doctor's Surgery.
"You shouldn't be out at your age!"
Said the receptionist.

"I know," I said,
"But it's embarrassing enough
Getting someone to hold the pot
While I pee in it,
Without expecting them to carry it
All the way up here!"

24th April 2020

Pastel Morning haiku

Over the rooftops
And across a silent sea
A pastel morning

8th April 2020

Miss England tanka

Miss England returns
Doctor Bhasha Mukherjee
Self isolating

Then back to the hospital
Beauty and Duty combined

7th April 2020

Silver Sea haiku

Sometime in the night
Some Angel laid soothing hands
On our silver sea

5th April 2020

Res J. F. Burman

Ann's Gardens

You'd think that she was praying
Down there on her knees
Paying close attention
To everything she sees
Her fingers busy scrabbling
Among the plants and dirt
And she spends so long bowed over
You know her back must hurt!

But you know that it's all worth it
When you see her gardens bloom
And the flowers shine so brightly
They'd banish any gloom
And all the scents and perfumes
That waft up in the air
You'd think that Ann's created
A piece of Heaven there!

She has always had a garden
No matter where she goes,
She's always planting something
And tending Father's rose.
And when her labour's over
She loves to go and see
The result of all her endeavours
With an evening G and T.

I think this is how Ann worships
Creating beauty for the eyes
And whatever prayers she mutters
Must surely reach up to the skies
And she blends these lovely perfumes
Without Frankincense or Myrrh
I'm sure the God of all the Gardens
Must be so well pleased with her.

25th July 2020

Coloured Lights haiku

I burn coloured lights
Shining into our darkness
Workers wending home

4th April 2020

Coughing tanka

When I start coughing
I remind myself sternly
Stay away from chillies

Self isolate from the stove
When hot chillies hit hot oil

3rd April 2020

Polished haiku

Sometimes it appears
As though a huge giant hand
Has polished our seas

3rd April 2020

Two Metre Separation haiku

That is not allowed
Never mind taking the piss
You are far too close

2nd April 2020

If I Go Away haiku

If I go away
Keep a light in the window
So I'll know you're there

2nd April 2020

Today a Pigeon haiku

Today a pigeon
The first bird in my backyard
Since before Christmas

1st April 2020

Ready for the fray haiku

The world emerges
Battleship grey and silver
Ready for the fray

31st March 2020

Setsubun haiku

Cold kiss of the wind
In Japan it's Setsubun
Last day of winter

3rd February 2020

The Sentry haiku

Keeping watch for cats
The Sentry... poised and alert
Whilst his partners feed

26th November 2019

When We Were Young

It is the same moon
That lit our faces, entwined hands
When we loved each other

When every touch and sigh
Was a wonder, a miracle
And a revelation

It is the same moon
That touched our hearts
When we were young

10th January 2012

Friday 13th December 2019

Before 1948 and the founding of our National Health Service suicide among the elderly was common.
Without a Welfare State many feared "becoming a burden" upon their childrenand chose to end their lives!
I fear we return to those "Good Old Days!"

Democracy has been crucified upon the Cross of Lies!
Honesty has been sold to the highest bidder!
Compassion has been sacrificed upon the Altar of Self Interest!
Truth has been washed away by the torrent of hatred!
Brotherhood has been consumed by xenophobia!
Like vermin from the gutter, those who fucked dead pigs
And burnt fifty pound notes in front of the homeless,
Jostle once again at the trough!

Once again Parliament will try to suppress the unions,
Pass laws to outlaw protest and free speech.
Goodwill to be dismissed as a Communist Plot.
Kindness will be seen as the Loonie Left
And Love? Well who will have time or energy for that
When "heat or eat" are upmost on so many minds!

So preventable deaths will rise,
Homelessness will multiply,
Child Poverty will increase,
Food Banks will run out of food,
Suicide will become a way of life!
Our Nurses will be pushed aside
And probably blamed for the crisis
In our Privatised National Wealth Service.
"For the few, but not the many!"

Schools will teach "He who lies wins!"
On their slates when they can't afford paper.
Islanders will drown as the oceans rise
The Cayman Islands will sink into the sea
Under the weight of Ill Gotten Gains!
And as our planet dies you can all say,
"It can't be my fault. I voted Tory!"

May all your Gods and Goddesses forgive you!

I never will!
When Suicide becomes
Once more,
A way of life!

13th December 2019

Sunlit Castle haiku

The Sunlit Castle
Floats above a choppy sea
Winter storms out there

6th December 2019

Dusk haiku

Just before dusk falls
The colours change for the night
So we'll miss them more

1st December 2019

Aerial Aviator haiku

An Aviator
Flying low past my window
Strange sights in Penwith

26th November 2019

Cornish November haiku

Hurricane force winds
Flood warnings and roads blocked
Normal for Cornwall

2nd November 2019

Morning Visitor haiku

Braving hungry cats
And storm tossed waving bamboo
Morning visitor

31st October 2019

It's That Sort of Day haiku

It's that sort of day
When the rain travels sideways
Winter starts early

29th October 2019

Chinese Seasons Frost Descends haiku

The scent of Jasmine
In my small concrete back yard
Autumn Frost Descends

28th October 2019

The Penzance Lineman gogyoshi

Penzance calling...
Penzance calling... are you there
I guard your telephone wires
And your internet fibre-optics
I am the Penzance Jackdaw lineman

12.7.2019

Summer Sunshine tanka

The summer sunshine
Melting the tar on the roads
Friendly neighbours pass

Sunblock wafts upon the air
The pigeons are still cooing

25th June 2019

Mountain Airs haiku

Pilgrim soul weary
Burned dry by the summer sun
Dreams of Mountain airs

25th June 2019

Res J. F. Burman

The Pub Cat haiku

After a hard night
In the boozer... the pub cat
Sleeps it off outside

18.6.2019

Norfolk Island Pine II haiku

Norfolk Island Pine
Weeping for its sunny home
In the Southern Seas

4th June 2019

Night Cramps

Argh... your cry of pain
Propelled from your bed
By the agony of cramps
In your lower legs and feet!

It feels as though
Your shins and calves
Are being crushed
In some medieval torture device!

Your feet are bunched
Like boxer's fists
As you stamp stampstamp
Trying to pop the bones
Back into their allotted place!

You dive into the bedside drawer
Looking for some Quinine
But the blister pack is empty
Victim of previous attacks.
So now you set off
Again on clenched feet
Staggering downstairs
In search of more Quinine.

You're half naked
So must do all this in the dark
Lest you frighten the neighbours

Or the wildlife!

Ah, open a fresh packet
Of Quinine Sulphate
It says take one at night
But this is the second and needed!

Back to bed
Still trying to stretch
Those calf muscles
Pulling up one's toes
To stretch some more!

Then it occurs to you
"Shoulda taken some Arnica
That's gonna bruise!"
But it's too late now!

And so you lie there
Contemplating the indignities
That Age inflicts upon this body
That I still dream is young and virile!

This is all down to bad planning!
I thought I'd live fast
Die young and leave a beautiful memory.
I didn't know I had to plan for all this!

5th June 2019

Today I'm Blue!

For today I lost a friend,
A fellow poet and brother
And an Oh so human being.
So today I am blue!

I should be grateful
For his release
From cancer and pain.
But I'll do that tomorrow,
For today I am blue.

I should rejoice
At his friendship,
So freely given.
But today I cannot
Because today I am blue!

I should exalt
At the fun we shared
Colluding and duelling
With poetic words.
But that must wait,
For today I am so blue!

I should applaud
His art and his music
His poetry and his kindness
But I must shelve that for the moment
Because today I am blue!

I should celebrate our friendship
The kindnesses he showed me
His humour
And his cutting wit.
But that must be delayed.
For my eyes are clouded with tears
And today I am blue!

Yes, today I am blue,
For my old mate has gone.
Soma Dog, Cerberus,

My Ol' Melbourne Bluesman
Has gone to pastures new.
I will celebrate his being,
But, sadly, not today
For my heart is breaking
And I am so so blue!

*Dedicated with the greatest affection to my old friend
Phillip Barker, The Soma Dog, Cerberus, my beloved friend!*

11th June 2019

Door Stepping a haiku chain

I was born to sit
In the evening sunshine
On my front door step

A Gin and Tonic
Sheltering in the shadow
Cast by the door frame

A Reporter's Pad
And a sharp Blackwing pencil
Old John Steinbeck's pride

Small moments of peace
Feed my creativity
And ease my old bones

These moments of peace
Need to be stored and cherished
Lest the winter comes

8th June 2019

Rainy Day haiku

It's that sort of day
Rain clings to the washing line
No laundry today

4th June 2019

Res J. F. Burman

Love's Ambassadors haiku

Dogs remember friends
They're always pleased to see them
Love's ambassadors

31.5.2019

Sea Fever haiku

Give me a tall ship
And a star to sail fer by
Masefield's Sea Fever.

A tribute to John Masefield and his wonderful poem "Sea Fever"

28th May 2019

The Carrion Crow haiku

Sure and confident
Feeding in the bladderwrack
The carrion crow

27th May 2019

Heaven's Messenger haiku

The white dove visits
And brings peace to my small world
Heaven's messenger?

25th May 2019

A Jackdaw haiku

The wary jackdaw
The morning sun polishing
His shiny feathers

23rd May 2019

Night Mist haiku

The night mist's moisture
Cascade down over the hills
Home to the ocean

22.5.2019

Godolphin Hill haiku

Godolphin hill floats
Upwards on a sea of mist
Reaching for heaven

22.5.2019

May Dawn haiku

May dawn's early light
Reveals a safe anchorage
Peaceful thoughts take flight

21.5.2019

Forever Young a tanka

When first I saw you
T'wassixty two years ago
So long I've loved you

But I see in my mind's eye
You are still forever young

1st May 2019

A Hungry Jackdaw haiku

A hungry jackdaw
More welcome than he can guess
Visits my backyard

1st May 2019

The Year of the Ox a tanka

The year of the ox
Bought me laughter, love and loss
So I took up arms

In the year of the tiger
Fifty seven long years ago

1st May 2019

Dreaming II a tanka

You lie beside me
But only when I'm dreaming
Your soft sweet kisses

Still caressing in my sleep
But where are you when I wake?

1st May 2019

Dreaming tanka

Sometimes I still dream
Of your sweet beloved face
Did I not tell you

I would love you forever
Or until the seas run dry

30th April 2019

Eagle Screams a haiku

The Eagles still scream
The names of the Tribal Gods
Who is left to hear?

24.4.2019

Primroses haiku

Quiet companions
Down here among the gravestones
Where primroses lie

23rd April 2019

Mercy tanka

Here I sit below
The Goddess and Dear Lao Tzu
Praying for mercy

That my old friend may be well
And remain with us a while

21st April 2019

Bosoms and Halter Tops haiku

I love the summer
When bosoms and halter tops
Burst out everywhere

20th April 2019

Panama Hat haiku

Last week was winter
Today's so hot it's high time
For my Panama

20th April 2019

Evening G & T haiku

Evening G & T
Sitting on my front doorstep
Sunshine fills my heart

19th April 2019

I Wish I Were....

I wish I was in Singapore
Now it's winter here
I wish I was in Holland Village
Sitting in the Square.

I wish I was in Haw Paw Villa
Seeing all those statues there
I love Tiger Balm gardens
With sea breezes in my hair.

I wish I was in Old Penang
Those temples for to see
And pretty girls would bring me drinks
And make a fuss of me.

I wish I was in Santubong
Where the Palm Trees gently sway
And clouds form like smoke rings
Around the islands in the bay.

I wish I was in Jesselton
Before it changed its name
I'd climb the Sacred Mountain
Just to see that view again.

I wish I was back in Bau
Where the girls with dimples play
I'd go swimming in the Gold Mine
And eat market food all day.

I wish I was in Kuching
Eating in the Market Place
Where the girls are all so pretty
And there's a smile on every face.

Yes, I wish I was in Kuching
Eating MeeHoon in the square
Chatting with all my old friends
Who I used to meet down there.

cont.

I wish I was in Sibu
Around regatta time
We'd eat and drink so hearty
With those old friends of mine.

I wish I was in Sarawak
To see in Chinese New Year
We'd eat and drink and party
With the old friends I hold so dear!

13th April 2019

Valentine's Day haiku

Valentine's Day
My heart turns to all lost loves
Warming my sadness

14th February 2019

Kuching haiku

Dreams of Old Kuching
And my days in Sarawak
Still my heart lies there

8th February 2019

Keep Your Hammer Face Polished

My Uncle Piers was a gentle man
Though he fought in World War One
He never breathed a word about it
After he and the War were done!

He should have been a carpenter
And his water colours give me a thrill
And his words were full of wisdom
And I remember them so well still.

My Uncle always told me
When I was nothing but a kid,

"Keep your hammer face polished
It'll save you many a quid!"

"A clean hammer face will always strike true
Never glance off the nail,
It'll save you many handles
And many blackened fingernails!"

"Keep your chisels fiercely sharp
And all your knife blades too
A blunt blade is the dangerous one
A sharp blade will serve you true!"

"And always set your saw teeth
So carefully to left and to right
You'll find you need to sharpen less
And the cut won't pinch you tight!"

"And always have a pot of grease
To dip your screws, to hand
Think of the man who unscrews them
In another age or other land!"

I still have his pre-war Chisels
His planes and his saw setting tools
They are as precious to me as when I was three
When he taught me his golden rules.

My Uncle Piers was a gentle man
And my Aunty Ivy was pretty and sweet
She made the best custard I ever did taste
And was the nicest person you ever could meet!

1st November 2018

November Mornings haiku

November morning
Bring their threats and promises
We shall accept both

1.11.2018

The Great West Road

I've travelled this old road
For oh so many years
Travelled in both directions
Through laughter and through tears

I remember when it was
Almost a country road
When lorries hit the houses
Or scraped them with their loads

I've travelled it by lorry
I've travelled it by car
I've walked it in the summer heat
When my feet stuck to the tar.

I've walked the moors in icy cold
The snow blowing in my eyes
I've carried my too heavy pack
Beneath the buzzard's cries

I've known this road from London
And every step to Land's End
I've known her like an enemy
I've known her as my friend

I've travelled it in the old way
With a Donkey and a cart
I've travelled it with laughter
And gone back with a broken heart

It's wended it's winding way
From London to the West
Since well before Roman times
And it's a road we love the best

For though we wander here and there
Across land and sea and foam
The Great West Road is the one we trust
To bring us all safe home.

31st October 2018

Haiku Road

I'd love to live on Haiku Road
Down the end of Basho Street
Where all the poets gather
And bow to all they meet!

There'd have to be a Temple
For the quiet of one's mind
And a cosy little tea house
With the best foods they could find.

And then we'd need some mountains
And some forests and bamboo
And quiet shady places
Where the spirit could renew.

Yes I want to live on Haiku Road
I think I'd love it there
And if not I'd move round the corner
And live in Tanka Square!

26th October 2018

Green for Gold haiku

Cold bites at the trees
As they consume their sugars
And swap green for gold

26th October 2018

Morning Sun haiku

Autumn morning sun
So low on the horizon
Dazzling my eyes

22nd October 2018

A Divine Hand haiku

Light on a tree trunk
Confirming the existence
Of a divine hand

17th October 2018

Waning Days haiku

Every falling leaf
Still echoes summer's beauty
Autumn's waning days

17th October 2018

The Conservative Party Conference haiku

Theresa May danced
On the graves of Dead Britons
Austerity kills

4th October 2018

Sparkling Waters haiku

Under the dark clouds
Autumn sunshine still appears
On sparkling waters

24th September 2018

Fools Knocking haiku

It's that sort of day
Autumn chill bites my old bones
Fools knock on my door

22nd September 2018

Michelle

Look at this young maid.
She looks perfect, doesn't she?
I thought she was perfect!
But alas, No!
Life is like that, isn't it!
Full of disappointments!
I went out to celebrate
Losing 18 kilos!
And what did pretty Michelle do?
She started to make me
A SMALL cappuccino!
A SMALL cappuccino?
For crissakes,
I'm a man of appetites!
Can't she see that?
So, as I said,
Life is full of small disappointments!
But she is still
A Sweetheart,
Don't you think?

9th October 2014

Away with the Birds haiku

There are some that say
I am away with the birds
A divine madness

19th September 2018

Bowing haiku

Autumn wind and rain
Attack the bowing bamboo
Never losing grace

15th September 2015

Trishaw Man haiku

Prince or trishaw man
To every worthy child
Their father is king

13th September 2018

The Garlic Revolution gogyoshi

The recipe demanded
That the garlic be crushed!
I am pleased to report
The garlic has been smashed!
Resistance was futile!

6th September 2018

Autumn Airs gogyoshi

Autumn airs bring a chill
To my old bones
And my left foot
Which has no feeling
Or big toe nail.... aches!

30th August 2018

Come Away!

There's a ship the bay
And she's calling my name
Come sail on the Ocean
Across the broad main.

Come pack up your gear
And bid loved ones to bide
For the wind it is freshening
And we sail on the tide.

Let's seek out adventure
Some new tales to tell
New places to trade

Strange new things to sell.

Let's sail round the islands
Before we're too old
Perhaps we'll come back
With treasure and gold!

They say we're sea farers
Since the dawn of time
Be it small local lugger
Or a ship of the line.

We've salt in our veins
And there's tar on our hands
Let's once more away
And seek foreign lands.

And if I find I'm too old
Or I do not have the means
 I will still sail the oceans
On a ship of my dreams!

24th August 2018

Denver Scanes gogyoshi

My old friend Denver Scanes
His cheery greetings
Still ring in my ears
"Hello Sailor" and "Love Ya Man"
Still whisper from my telephone!

Rest in Peace Denver "The Dude" Scanes
1949 ~ 2016

21st August 2018

Skirmishing with The Little 'C'

I've danced with Death a time or two
And so far come off best
But there's no kind of certainty
That I'll always pass the test.

I've skirmished with the best of 'em
Picked up a scar or two
Had a close encounter with a bayonet
But it didn't run me through.

I've been peppered by mortar shells
But it just was not my time
And picked up the odd ball bearing
From my own side's Claymore mine.

I've heard Death's deadly whisper
In the bullet's whiplash crack
And as I ducked away from it
Felt his fingers on my back!

I nearly drowned in the River Camel
In Doom Bar's spiteful rip
And in a flat bottomed Landing Craft
In a Cyclone's fearful grip!

But these are only little scratches
Beside two lovers who must part
For there are few wounds deeper
Than those of a broken heart!

But now I face the Surgeon's knife
And if it's so... I must
It's a little like surrender
When you take so much on trust.

But trust's a thing that will carry you
Through many a scrape or fight
When you rely on the man beside you,
At your six and left and right.

So trust I shall, the Surgeons hand

It's cunning and its skill
The Nurses tender care will pull
Me through... I trust it will.

But if, perchance, my time is up
And Death is hovering near,
Well Death is just an old old friend
And one I do not fear!

I would not rage against the night
As many think we should
I've had a long and loving life
And trust my death'll be as good!

12th August 2018

Rain tanka

I see the heatwave
Has broken... rain cools hot earth
Huddled figures rush

My view is hidden by rain
But still my Post Lady smiles

*Dedicated to Sarah, my Post Lady
whose smile lights up the day.*

11th August 2018

Politics two haiku

Trump and Kim Jong Un
Children in small men's bodies
Take away their toys

Kim Jong Un and Trump
Spoiled children badly in need
Of a good spanking

9th August 2017

Collared Doves haiku

Doves in these town streets
Still coo like the wood pigeons
Of my woodland home

9th August 2015

Seeking the Shadows haiku

Seeking the shadows
Father protects his young son
From summer's fierce heat

5th August 2018

Precious Moment haiku

Sweet eyes filled with tears
Parting's sorrow overflows
Oh precious moment

23rd May 2018

Gentle Rain haiku

A gentle rain falls
On the great and small alike
The smell of summer

21st July 2018

Saint Crispin's Day haiku

Be gentle with me
I whispered too quietly
It fell on deaf ears

21st July 2018

John Steinbeck's Pencil haiku

Blackwing 602
Half the pressure, twice the speed
John Steinbeck's pencil

19th July 2018

Scribbler's Delight haiku

John Steinbeck's fav'rite
A Palomino Blackwing
A scribbler's delight

19th July 2018

Bad Planning

It's all down to Bad Planning!
I thought that I'd live fast,
Die young
And leave a beautiful memory!

But plans went awry.
I'm now too old to die young!
And even my memory
Is already fading!

They say that old age
Never arrives unaccompanied!
It brings all this other crap
Along with it!

So the aches and pains,
These tumours and diabetes,
These difficulties breathing
And peeing.

Are all down to Bad Planning
Not Old Age at all
Because... believe it or not,
I'm getting younger every day!

17th July 2018

Evening Musings haiku and tanka

Evening sun warm
Upon my old aching bones
Green tea from the East

Pilgrim soul at rest
Summer sun shines on my step
Now seems far enough

Too old to wander
Yet this summer breeze stirs me
Gypsy in my soul

I have seen such scenes
As sun rises on jungles
Seen the Hornbill fly

Listened to the Gibbon's calls
Like birdsong among the trees

11th June 2018

Foxgloves Await haiku

After the night's rain
Foxgloves await the sunshine
So that bees may feed

6th June 2018

Buddha's Care haiku

Young bamboo reaches
Up towards the summer sky
Under Buddha's care

6th June 2018

Res J. F. Burman

TickaTacka haiku

Even at my age
We old Hippies still love some
Ol' Flower Power

5th June 2018

Headache haiku

Thunderstorm Warning
Headache racks it up a notch
Paracetamol

4th June 2018

Foxgloves haiku

Foxgloves wait in vain
No fox will come to wear these
My small back-street yard

4th June 2018

Bamboo haiku

Early morning sun
Watching my bamboo growing
Summer's here at last

4th June 2018

True Friendship

Even as petals start to fall
The fragrance of true friendship
Lingers
And will last forever more!

31st May 2018

Alsatian Puppy haiku

Alsatian Puppy
On the step licking my ear
Hail Old Soul... Well met

2017

Paddy haiku

I wonder
Is sixty years too long
To miss you

21st September 2017

Young Once haiku

I too was young once
And over the years I found
Once was quite enough

17th September 2017

Hindu Jewel haiku

Walking through Neasden
I see sparkling in sunshine
A Hindu Jewel

The sight of BAPS Shri Swaminarayan Mandir in Neasden.

14th September 2017

Autumn Glory haiku

Her hair was a blaze
Of Autumn Glory.... shining
Like a new dawn day

12th September 2017

Autumn Airs

Autumn airs descend
And all the trees are sighing
The song of the mist

Autumn rains...
The earth smells rich and deep and
Grateful

9th September 2012

Red Mugs

I read that brewing tea
In a Red Mug
Makes the tea
Taste sweeter

But brewing my tea
In a Red Mug
That says
"Keep Calm
You're only 40"
Makes me feel
Much Younger!

9th September 2017

The East is Always Calling tanka

Leave cold tears behind
The East is always calling
Like breeze through bamboo

I yearn for quiet temples
And busy market places

1st September 2017

845 NACS haiku

The whupwhupwhupwhup
Of those helicopter blades
Magic carpet home

31st August 2017

With grateful thanks to the crews of 845 Naval Air Commando Squadron.
Unlike some in the Borneo conflict, they came when they were needed and flew with courage and amazing skill.
There are many Soldiers and Marines alive today
due to these brave men!
Thank You.

Going to Market haiku

It has been hard work
Going to market each week
But now I'm sailing

31st August 2017

Alms haiku

Those who have little
Understand hunger and need
Live with open hands

31st August 2017

Tall Bamboo haiku

She heard him singing
In the tall bamboo forest
And her heart grew wings

1st August 2017

Jungle Patrol haiku

Watch your six he said
Glancing over his shoulder
But death lay ahead

30th August 2017

Eagles haiku

Johnny Cash sang it
"Like a mighty rush of Eagles!
Wish I'd written that

4th September 2017

The Earth Pin

It flashed around the Radio Net
With the speed of Summer Lightning
That we'd lost another comrade
And this time not due to fighting.

I'm sure they taught him better
And I'm sure they drummed it in
That never, never, never
Should you piss on your own earth pin.

It's nothing to do with hygiene
Nor to limit your liberty
But pissing on your earth pin
Improves its conductivity.

Those 3 ton radio wagons
Running through the tropic night
Build up a lot of static
Lookin' for somewhere to alight.

Maybe he was just tired
Was it sleepiness that done him in?
But training should have taken over
Never piss on your own earth pin.

cont.

The news flashed round the units
On the tragic night he died,
He pissed upon his earth pin
And that was why he fried!

Oh what a waste of training
But he's the one we blames
The young soldier should always
Be careful where he aims!

The Army may lead a man astray
Tempt him with many a sin
But never should you ever
Piss on your own earth pin!

28th August 2017

Pneumonia a tanka

Pneumonia struck
And put an end to summer...
Autumn in August

Still the sparrows feed their young
The seagulls wake up screaming

27th August 2015

Greek Steps haiku

I follow the walls
Keeping within the shadows
Greek summer sunshine

21st August 2017

Basho's Grave haiku

Here Basho still sleeps
But his words whisper to me
Sweet summer longing

23rd August 2017

Jungle haiku chain

Here is a jungle
Dripping wet with summer rain
Outside my window

But no longhouses
No Iban or Dayak maids
No one head-hunting

Just a Cornish yard
And Bamboos in flower pots
And dreams of my youth

24th August 2017

Yorkshire Tea haiku

*I seldom have anything nice to say about Yorkshire.
That damned county tried to kill me several times
back in the winter of 1962-63
in Catterick Camp.*

*Not that I'm an unforgiving sorta chap
it's just that I do know how to hold a grudge!
Anyway....*

Brewed for five minutes
Two tea bags in a Red Cup
Yorkshire Tea ~ Gold Blend

23rd August 2017

Red Threads tanka

The Chinese believe
There are Red Threads tying us
To our destinies

Our friends - our loves - all we know
Bound close to us forever

22nd August 2017

Kisses

There are some eyes
That seem to look right into your soul.
There are some faces
That remain in your soul forever.

There are some hands
Whose slightest touch
Feels like a kiss
Upon your lips.

There are some necks
Made to worship and admire.
Some skin that seems to shine
With the kisses the sun laid upon it.

There are some lips…..

21st August 2017

Hero Monks haiku

Old Chinese Folklore
Often tells of flying monks
Heroes of the way

20th August 2017

Seagull haiku

Seagull
Like a flying handkerchief
Blown across the bay

20th August 2012

Shy Smile haiku

One shared cup of tea
A shy smile across the room
And then you were gone

19th August 2017

Bonzo & Lobo haiku

Dreaming of my friends
And the void they left behind
No dogs to lick my tears

19th August 2012

Bonzo haiku

My old friend Bonzo
I'd wait at the station forever
If I thought he'd come home

19th August 2012

Longan Harvest haiku

The touch of her hand
Adds sweetness and flavour
To the fruit she picks

19th August 2017

Oh Barcelona haiku

Oh Barcelona
I keep my tears to myself
But send you my Love

18th August 2017

Fire haiku

Her hair shone like fire
Or New England autumn woods
A blaze of glory

17th August 2017

Holstered Pistol haiku

I saw the photo
Holstered Pistol on her hip
Wild Child... so long gone

17th August 2017

Robin Williams haiku

Robin Williams
If only I could reach out
Lift one small sorrow

17th August 2017

*Robin Williams 21 Jul 1951 - 11 Aug 2014
Still Loved and Missed!*

Tweeting haiku

I don't ever tweet
Summer Autumn or Winter
Leave it to the birds

16th August 2017

Bamboos droop haiku

Bamboos droop and drip
Bowed down by weight of water
British Summer Time

16 August 2012

Lavender Lady haiku

Lavender Lady
Your face kissed by faint freckles
Grace in every move

15th August 2017

Brompton Road haiku chain

That tiny bed-sit
Above Brompton Cemetery
My many young dreams

Below my window
An old lady tends a grave
All hopes and dreams flown

Just off Brompton Road
My bohemian love nest
Just six pounds a week

Saturdays up West
In folk clubs and jazz cellars
London's winter scene

On Sunday mornings
Drinking Maxwell House coffee
From old coffee jars

Poring over maps
Planning next summer's journeys
Farewell lovemaking

On every journey
The horizon beckoned me
Come… come… come away

So the road call'd me
While one small part looked backwards
Farewell Brompton Road

16th August 2012

Tidying Up

Have you ever started tidying up
And kept on finding things
That needed a special place.
Ten years worth of eye-glasses
With matching tinted versions
That need their own box.

And bills and bank statements
That need checking for PPI payments.
And pencils worn too short to use
But still too good to throw away!
And a penknife with a thing to take
Boy Scouts out of horse's hooves.

And foreign stamps that you've put aside
For someone, but you can't remember
Which box they live in!
There's boxes that wrist watches came in
And one full of foreign coins.
Rolls of double-sided sticky tape
In case you ever get invited to appear
On Blue Peter.

Rolls of sticky address labels
For the last house not this one!

A Japanese Lacquer and Mother of Pearl box
With slips of paper with a Chinese God on them.
"Wei T'o, Protector of Books.
Insures against fire, destructive insects
And
Dishonest borrowers!"
Which I stick in the frontispiece
Of all my books.
Usually works!

A Monocular, in a belt pouch
That I've been looking for
Forever!

Two boxes with sliding lids

Each containing two pairs
Of Chop sticks.
Very hard to open
No wonder the Chinese are all so thin.

A large wallet
Containing an out-of-date Passport
Discharge Papers from the Army
"Assessments of Military Conduct and Character"
"Exemplary"
I must have fooled somebody!
A very old Birth Certificate
Circa 1942
And my old medals!

Some Chinese Lucky Money Envelopes
And some Hell Banknotes!
Millions of Dollars
Of money for the Dead!

My "Funeral Plan"
A large envelope containing
All the details of my funeral
Already bought and paid for
To save others the expense!

"The Way of Life
According to
Lao Tzu"
By Witter Bynner.
My favourite translation
Of the "Tao Te Ching"
My constant companion
Since I was in my twenties.

And Gibran's "The Prophet"
Travelling with me
Almost as long!
Two peacock feathers
And a set of brass divining rods.
Two pairs of Chinese Exercise Balls
That ring like chimes.
No, there's a third pair, smaller.

A nice little hexagonal bamboo box
With a wooden stash box inside.
But alas no stash!

Pencil boxes full of pencils
Worn too short to use
But still too good to throw away.
Now where did I put those other
Pencils?

There are no Gods or Goddesses here
I care for them better,
But there might be their footprints
In the dust.

An old Head-hunter's Mandu
Hanging by my chair
Still sharp enough to take a head
Or chop through thickest jungle.
A Gurkha Kukri
From my days with those
Gentle souls from the Mountains!

A carved box full of yet more pencils
Still haven't found the first lot!
And two little plastic tick lifters
For getting ticks off dogs.

There's a Chinese Water Pipe,
But without a tassel or the right tools.
People think they're Opium Pipes,
But that's just wishful thinking,
They're one-shot tobacco pipes!
I know what an Opium Pipe looks like!
But I don't have one.
Anymore!

Here's a Stanley knife,
Still sharp, because
I just cut my thumb on it!
I was looking for the bandage
I put on it, everywhere!
Finally, I found it floating

In the loo. Guess I can't
Use that one again!

And special cloths for cleaning
Your eyeglasses but
They're never large enough!

A tube of glue, set so hard
I might use it for a wedge
To keep the back door open.

At this point I turn around
And find all my tidying
Has wrecked my room.
Destroyed it utterly!
It's worse than when I started.

There are piles of papers
And boxes piled
All over the room!
Bags of shredded documents
And the shreds that escaped
On the Carpet!

And a foot has come off
My guillotine
And I just can't abide
A wobbly guillotine!
And I can't find my glasses!
They're not on my nose
And they're not on my forehead.
Where the f**k did I put
That cardboard box
Full of old eyeglasses?

I should have listened
To Dear Dorothy.
She says there's always
Better things to do
Than to clean and tidy!
I just know she's right!

Anybody want any
Very short pencils?

1st August 2015

Pine Straw

I love to rest on pine straw
Somewhere off the track
Where passersby won't see me
A pine tree at my back.

But all the woodland knows I'm there
The robin comes to sing
A Lady Blackbird cleans my boots
Or shares the food I bring.

Sister fox will wander by
And stop with enquiring stare
She sees I have no stick or gun
She knows there's no danger here.

The Badger won't be coming by
Unless I wait till dusk
But I can see the track they make
And sometimes smell their musk.

I can hear the buzzards cry
Circling high above
And soon they will be nesting
In these woodlands that I love.

But I am truly so aware
Of the very air I breathe
The moisture in the soil
The pollen on the breeze.

I breathe in all the goodness
I breathe out all the bile
It does a body's soul some good
To sit still for a while.

I love the songs that different trees
Are making on the air
Goddess of Mercy, if there's a Heaven
I believe it must be here!

18th September 2015

Strawberries and Cream

I'm eating Strawberries and cream
With my long-handled spoon
The one the doggies loved to lick.
I know I shouldn't but I don't care!

My beloved sister bought them.
I think they were meant for
A pretty little girl who was visiting
But she'd already eaten a punnet of strawberries
And half a plateful of biscuits!

Sweet child, she bought me a lovely bunch of flowers
And then decided they were so nice,
She should hold on to them!
See, she's pretty and clever too!

Never mind, my beloved sister
Bought me flowers from her garden
Which puts my little backyard to shame
I can smell the roses now from across the room.

And mauvy spikey things
That she did tell me the name of
But you know me, head like a colander!
And some pretty white flowers
That look like Christmas tree decorations.

And the strawberries and cream!
You can blame my next coronary on her!
But I won't! I love her too much!
And always have! Sweet Annabella!

And she didn't hold me down
And force them on me.
She hasn't been able to do that
Since I was ten years old!

Lovely to see my dear friend Eve
And Little-legs, full of smiles and strawberries.
And my Dear Sister and Brother-in-Law.
Yesterday was a good day, a very good day!

No One

No one to lick the mayonnaise
From my long-handled spoon,
Or eat the nub ends from my pasty
Or join me howling at the moon!

No one to help me to the bathroom
Or to lead me down the stairs,
No one to help me eat my supper
With long and hungry stares.

No one to help me on computer
Though he cannot type a damn
But he's growing up so nicely
A proper Penberthy man.

No one to snuggle against me
While lying on my bed,
Or wake me up too early
In case I might be dead!

No one is there to trip me up
On all the scattered toys,
But Babes, I must admit to you
Your Old Grandad misses his boys!

12th July 2015

Zhang Ziyi haiku

In my life's fading
There are some divine faces
Make me feel like spring

10th February 2015

Res J. F. Burman

This Country In Between

Every flower I send you
Is yet another kiss
Upon your lovely lips
Every petal I send you
Is a caress upon your soul
My body lying so close
You can feel my heat
And you will feel my love
All you have to do
Is reach out, connect
Bridge this tiny gap
This country in between
Complete the circuit
And when we finally touch
Twill be like fire
And twill be like ice
But every kiss upon your breast
Will be like a rose petal
Falling
Upon the ground it loves

25th December 2007

Singapore Customs

"What's this?" crowed the officious
British ex-pat Customs Officer.
Looking down at my Army Issue
Machete strapped to my battered
Army Issue suitcase.

"You can't bring that in 'ere!
That's a lethal weapon, that is!"

A more useless bit of kit is hard to imagine,
In its pressed cardboard sheath,
And its heavy riveted handle
That would cut and blister
A sweat soft hand to ribbons in minutes.
And it's impossible to sharpen edge
Could hardly be called lethal.

Unless you wanted to batter something to death
With its blunt edge!

"You can't bring that in 'ere,
That's a lethal weapon, that is!"

Luckily, he hadn't looked IN my suitcase!
He'd have found the Headhunter's mandu,
Razor sharp, the machete I really carried on ops,
With itsstylized hornbill handle with the beak
That curled round your little finger
And stopped the thing from flying out
Of a sweat wet or monsoon wet hand.
Or the quiver of poisoned blowpipe darts!
Now they really were lethal!

I wasn't in the best of moods!
I'd been kicked out of my beloved Borneo
At a moment's notice!
They'd thought to retain
My trusty 7.62 FN
But had returned my 'personal weapon'.
And found me a last-minute seat
On a Singapore Airlines flight!

And there I stood
In the bright lights of Singapore Airport.
Dirty, tired, in a pair of rotting jungle boots
And a set of Olive Greens
That hadn't seen starch
Or the dhobi man's iron
In far too long!
And I'd missed my tea!
And if this officious prat kept me much longer
It looked like I'd miss my supper too!

"You can't bring that in 'ere,
That's a lethal weapon, that is!"

"What the fuck do you call this?" I asked politely,
Pointing to the ugly little Sterling sub-machine gun
They'd returned to me before I left,
Hanging round my neck like the eternal albatross!

And the full magazines hanging from my belt!
"Souvenirs?"
For me, Peace had broken out!

10th October 2014

The Death of a Hooray Henry

She was an exquisite little flower,
And she never made a fuss,
When she hung about our billet,
And wanted to marry us!

But for once Old Tommy Atkins
Lived up to his better nature,
And we called her little sister,
And not a hand was laid upon her.

We gave her a camp bed in a corner,
And we guarded her that way,
And gave her little jobs to do,
So she could earn from day to day.

So she'd take and fetch our laundry
To the "Dhobi Girl' over the way,
And bring us mee hoon soup for tea,
And make herself useful every day.

And then some Hooray Henry,
Still white behind the knees,
Decided our little sister wasn't safe,
Among we licentious thieves!

So he had her taken to the Officers Mess,
And made her wait on tables, clean the silver plates.
And every night he'd fuck her,
And share her with his mates!

And then we heard him boasting,
How his little native whore,
Would suck and fuck him all night long
And still come back for more!

Last we heard of our little sister,
Who we'd protected for so long
She was broken and pregnant down by the docks,
And screwing for a song!

Our Hooray Henry didn't last,
Before his knees were brown ,
He died of snakebite to the groin
And in a monsoon ditch he was found!

And there's some that said we done it!
But that just could not be right,
Because our beloved Captain Harkabir swore,
We were all on duty with him that night!

So again, we licentious other ranks,
Proved what we had already sussed,
We were better men than the Public-School scum,
Sent out to govern us!

0545 Saturday 20th September 2014

Misty Dreams

The Magic Island
Is now lost in misty dreams
Of Autumn glories

18th September 2014

The Old Cormorant Fisherman

"What do you know of the modern world?"
I asked the Old Cormorant Fisherman,
Fishing in the same way
His Father and Grandfathers
Had before him for centuries.

He thought for a moment
And then replied comfortably,
"I know they still like to eat my fish!"

7th September 2014

Hanging Bookshelf

When there are no walls
Left for all your bookshelves
Hang them from a beam

25th August 2014

Rest in Peace, Robin Williams

Rest in Peace
Robin Williams
I liked you well
Thank you for all the laughter
I am sorry for all your pain!

August 2014

Bamboo Whispers haiku

When my lantern fails
Bamboos whisper directions
On my dark path home

17th July 2014

Why Do We Bother To Remember The Dead?

Why do we bother to remember the dead
Of all those wars, that even in our lifetimes
Are almost forgotten?
Why do we watch mealy mouthed politicians
Lay wreaths and make speeches
While they deny the survivors reasonable
Level of help, or treatment?

Better remember all those young men and women
As though they were alive.
What would they say about the state of the Veterans Hospitals?
The way the injured and traumatised are treated still.
What would they say about wars still being declared
By the rich and powerful who don't send their sons and daughters

Into harm's way?
Better remember all those executed
For cowardice or "Lack of Moral Fibre"
When they were suffering from Shell Shock!
No wonder they were traumatised
When their own country was determined to prove themselves
The real enemy that they had to fear!
Let us remember their families with nowhere to go!

What sort of countries would these young men and women
Have created had they not been thrown away
Discarded like the flowers of the forest
Before they had a chance of coming to full bloom
Would they have tolerated politicians and leaders
More interested in their own allowances
Than the welfare of veterans or serving soldiers?

If we are to remember our dead, not on one day
but on every day. Let us dedicate ourselves
to making the sacrifice of the dead worthwhile.
Let us ensure that if we send our young men to war
it be a just war. Not to make money for the few
but to ensure the safety of the many.
So that at last we should have countries fit for Hero's to Live In!

31st May 2010

Qǐngchīmǐfàn

Winnowing rice
Letting the wind work for you
Qing chi mifan

請吃米飯 = Qǐngchīmǐfàn = *Please eat [rice]*

25th July 20123

Res J. F. Burman

Fanning the Flames (For Niall O'Connor)

My new Fan
Nicknamed
The Towering
Deferno
Has broken
The heatwave.

Torrential rain
Floods
Thunder
And lightning
Are forecast.

And my new Fan
Waits
Remote Control
Poised
Eager for
The next
Hint of
Sunshine.

22nd July 2013

Another Young Friend Lost

Dedicated to
The Loving Memory
of
Jacob Cockle
Who drowned yesterday
(28th May 2013)
whilst photographing
Whirlpools from Underwater.
Jacob was a well-known surf photographer

Another Young Friend Lost

Another young friend lost.
We lose too many young people
Down here in the West.

If it's not illness
It's fast cars
On slow country lanes.
Or it's the waves
And the tides,
And our youth
So brave.
So talented and
So very brave.

Better perhaps
You had saved
Some of your bravery,
For your families,
And saved your lives!

Better perhaps you
Had saved some of your
Bravery.
For your Mothers
And your Fathers,
Sisters and Brothers
And all that loved you
Have greater need
Of that bravery now
Than you do.

By dying
You will now live
Forever young
In the hearts
That you leave behind.
Those hearts
In great need
Of your bravery
To sustain them
In their loss.

So brave but
Brokenhearted!

Rest in Peace.

29th May 2013

Shopkeeper

I always tell
My local shopkeeper
That old Chinese proverb

Man without smile should never open shop!
For some reason he doesn't seem to like it
Just highly strung, I guess.

18.5.2013

Spring haiku

So cold this spring
Almost June and even weeds
Struggle to prosper

15th May 2013

The Wicked Witch

She told me she was a witch
And she did cast a certain dark magic
Painting herself with a false glamour
And a certain genteel need.

But eventually the magic blew away
Like stale chaff on the wind
Redolent with the smell of rot
Leptospirosis and dirty ashtrays

Revealing a face scarred with avarice
Carefully manicured nails grasping
The genteel need replaced by spite
And all-consuming greed.

She told me she craved the company
Of old soldiers, loving the smell
Of sweet gun oil on sunburned skin
The faint whiff of cordite and adrenaline

But it was our stories she wanted
To steal them and adopt them as her own
So that the seven stone weakling appear giant
A 'Rupert'… a born leader of men!

When I gave her no stories of blood
She stole, instead, my money
Eleven Thousand Pounds credit
On which I still pay interest!

Eleven thousand pounds
Of my son's inheritance, who never did her wrong
And she thinks herself worthy to lecture
On Honour and Integrity?

She told me in her own land
She was a Princess. But in my land
Her own words label her LIAR
Her actions brand her THIEF

I am only a crippled old soldier
And my sins are too many to name
But I never stole from comrade or lover
Give me back my "shilling a day"!

Like the pi-dogs of the desert
She scavenged behind the march
But she's not welcome in the camp
And she is unfit
To sit
At my small fire

13th May 2013

Index

845 NACS haiku	78
A Divine Hand haiku	66
A Hungry Jackdaw haiku	58
A Jackdaw haiku	57
A Quiet Moment a haiku	29
Acceptance a haiku	21
Aerial Aviator haiku	51
Alms haiku	78
Alsatian Puppy haiku	76
Angel's Wing a gogyoshi	32
Ann's Gardens	47
Another Young Friend Lost	100
Another Young Friend Lost	99
Are You There	20
A-sailing a haiku	23
Ash Wednesday a haiku	35
Autumn Airs gogyoshi	68
Autumn Airs	77
Autumn Equinox haiku	45
Autumn Glory haiku	76
Away with the Birds haiku	67
Bad Planning	73
Bamboo haiku	75
Bamboos droop haiku	84
Basho's Grave haiku	80
Before Dawn a haiku	29
Better Days Coming a haiku	24
Blackwing haiku	45
Blood Red Dawn a haiku	29
Blue a haiku	21
Bonzo haiku	83
Bonzo& Lobo haiku	83
Bosoms and Halter Tops haiku	60
Bounty of the Seas gogyoshi	40
Bowing haiku	67
Breakfast a haiku	29
Brompton Road haiku chain	85
Buddha's Care haiku	74
Calm haiku	44
Chimneys of Battlefields haiku	41
Chinese Seasons Frost Descends haiku	52

Cold Sea haiku	42
Cold Still Clings a haiku	26
Collared Doves haiku	72
Coloured Lights haiku	48
Come Away!	68
Cornish November haiku	51
Cornwall My Home a haiku	25
Coronavirus	46
Coughing tanka	48
Covid jab haiku	41
Dancing in the Dark a gogyoshi	33
Dawn Confirms a haiku	22
De Gallant haiku	45
Denver Scanes gogyoshi	69
Denver Scanesa gogyoshi	42
Door Stepping a haiku chain	56
Dragon in the mist haiku	41
Dragon Sleeps haiku	43
Dragon's Resting a haiku	36
Dreaming II a tanka	59
Dreaming tanka	59
Dusk haiku	51
Eagle Screams a haiku	59
Eagles haiku	79
Echoing Footsteps a haiku	38
Evening G & T haiku	60
Evening Musings haiku and tanka	74
Every Cloud a haiku	24
Excited Insects a haiku	30
Fanning the Flames (For Niall O'Connor)	99
February Blues a haiku	37
Fever	22
Fifty Shades a haiku	37
Fire haiku	83
Fishermen a haiku	23
Flights of Fancy haiku	38
Fog haiku	41
Fools Knocking haiku	66
Forever Young a tanka	58
Foxgloves Await haiku	74
Foxgloves haiku	75
Friday 13th December 2019	50
Funeral	20

Gentle Rain haiku	72
Gloomy Weather a haiku	30
Glory a haiku	22
Glowering Clouds a gogyoshi	26
Glowering Clouds a haiku	28
Goddess Grant a haiku	23
Godolphin Hill a haiku	23
Godolphin Hill haiku	58
God's Canvas a tanka	25
Going to Market haiku	78
Greek Steps haiku	80
Green for Gold haiku	65
Guiding Light haiku	39
Haiku Road	65
Hanging Bookshelf	97
Headache haiku	75
Heaven a haiku	28
Heaven's Messenger haiku	57
Hero Monks haiku	82
Hindu Jewel haiku	76
Holstered Pistol haiku	84
Hope a haiku	33
Hope haiku	44
Hope on the Skyline a haiku	25
Hunger Games haiku	39
I Wish I Were....	61
If I Go Away haiku	48
Interesting Times	18
Introductions.	13
It's That Sort of Day haiku	52
John Steinbeck's Pencil haiku	73
Jungle haiku chain	81
Jungle Patrol haiku	79
Keep Your Hammer Face Polished	62
Kisses	82
Kuching haiku	62
Lavender Lady haiku	84
Life's Longing for Itself a haiku	24
Lockdown Isolation haiku	43
Lonesome Cry a haiku	27
Longan Harvest haiku	83
Love's Ambassadors haiku	57
Magic Moment a haiku	23

Maiden's Blush a haiku	19
May Dawn haiku	58
Mercy tanka	60
Michelle	67
Miss England tanka	46
Mist a gogyoshi	21
Mist a tanka	31
Mist and Rain haiku	40
Misty Dreams	96
Mongolia a gogyoshi	35
Monochrome a tanka	26
Monterey Pine a gogyoshi	34
Morning Cold haiku	44
Morning Sun haiku	65
Morning Sunshine a haiku	33
Morning Visitor haiku	51
Morning's Light a tanka	19
Mountain Airs haiku	52
My Last Will and Testament a tanka	37
Night Cramps	53
Night Mist haiku	58
No One	92
No View haiku	40
Norfolk Island Pine II haiku	53
North East Wind haiku	44
November Eyes a haiku	19
November Mornings haiku	63
Oh Barcelona haiku	83
Oh the Sunshine a haiku	33
Other Worlds a haiku	30
Oyster a haiku	25
Paddy haiku	76
Pale Sun haiku	43
Panama Hat haiku	60
Pastel Morning haiku	46
Pastel Promises haiku	42
Patch of Blue tanka	44
Peace a tanka	26
Peckish a haiku	24
Pine Straw	90
Pneumonia a tanka	80
Police Violence a gogyoshi	27
Polished a haiku	27

Polished haiku	48
Politics two haiku	71
Poppy haiku	45
Precious Moment haiku	72
Primroses haiku	60
Qīngchīmǐfàn	98
Rain tanka	71
Rainy Day haiku	56
Rays a tanka	31
Ready for the fray haiku	49
Red Mugs	77
Red Threads tanka	81
Remembered	21
Rest in Peace, Robin Williams	97
Revenge a haiku	37
Rise of Spring haiku	40
Robin Williams haiku	84
Roofs gogyoshi	39
Rudi a gogyoshi	31
Saint Crispin's Day haiku	72
Sand a tanka	33
Scribbler's Delight haiku	73
Sea Fever haiku	57
Seagull a haiku	31
Seagull haiku	82
Seagulls haiku	41
Seeking the Shadows haiku	72
Setsubun haiku	49
Shiver me Timbers a haiku	37
Shopkeeper	101
Showers a haiku	28
Shuttered Doors haiku	42
Shy Smile haiku	82
Silver Sea haiku	46
Singapore Customs	93
Skirmishing with The Little 'C'	70
Solitary Flight a haiku	31
Sound of the Waves a haiku	34
Sparkling Waters haiku	66
Spring haiku	101
St Piran's Day a haiku	30
St Valentine's Day a gogyoshi	36
Steam haiku	43

Stone Lantern a gogyoshi	39
Storm Clouds a haiku	20
Storms and Rain haiku	36
Strawberries and Cream	91
Summer Sunshine tanka	52
Sunbeams a haiku	36
Sunlight a haiku	30
Sunlit Castle haiku	51
Tall Bamboo haiku	78
The Bird a haiku	28
The Blues haiku	39
The Blues haiku	43
The Carrion Crow haiku	57
The Conservative Party Conference haiku	66
The Dawn	24
The Death of a Hooray Henry	95
The Earth Pin	79
The East is Always Calling tanka	77
The Garlic Revolution gogyoshi	68
The Great West Road	64
The Holy Headland a tanka	34
The Huffpost a gogyoshi	27
The Mount and the Dragon a gogyoshi	38
The Mount and the Dragon a haiku	35
The Mount haiku	40
The Old Cormorant Fisherman	96
The Old King a haiku	25
The Penzance Lineman gogyoshi	52
The Pilgrim a tanka	38
The Pub Cat haiku	53
The Sentry haiku	49
The Telephone Box a tanka	34
The Tennessee Waltz a tanka	35
The Wicked Witch	101
The Year of the Ox a tanka	59
This Country In Between	93
TickaTacka haiku	75
Tidying Up	86
Today a Pigeon haiku	49
Today I'm Blue!	55
Transatlantic Flight a tanka	19
Treasure a haiku	22
Trishaw Man haiku	68

True Friendship	75
Tweeting haiku	84
Two Gulls a haiku	35
Two Metre Separation haiku	48
Unforgiving Seas a haiku	36
Valentine's Day haiku	62
Waning Days haiku	66
Warmth a haiku	28
Waves	21
Wet Morning haiku	45
Wet Today	20
When We Were Young	49
Why Do We Bother To Remember The Dead?	97
Winter Requirements haiku	42
Women's Day a haiku	29
Yorkshire Tea haiku	81
Young Once haiku	76
Your Smile. An Ode to my Post Lady	32
Zhang Ziyi haiku	92

MAPublisher Catalogue

ISBN/Titles /Image/Author	ISBN/Titles /Image/Author	ISBN/Titles /Image/Author	ISBN/Titles /Image/Author
978-1-910499-00-9 Father to child By Mayar Akash	978-1-910499-08-5 HSJ Lakri Tura By Mayar Akash	978-1-910499-26-9 Colouring 1-10 By MAPublisher	978-1-910499-18-4 Basic Numbers 1-10 By MAPublisher
978-1-910499-16-0 River of Life By Mayar Akash	978-1-910499-09-2 HSJ Gilaf Procession By Mayar Akash	978-1-910499-27-6 Activity Numbers 1-10 By MAPublisher	978-1-910499-19-1 Number 1-100 By MAPublisher
978-1-910499-39-9 Eyewithin By Mayar Akash	978-1-910499-03-0 HSJ Mazar Sharif By Mayar Akash	978-1-910499-28-3 Activity Colouring Alphabets By MAPublisher	978-1-910499-20-7 Vowels By MAPublisher
978-1-910499-32-0 WG Survivor By Mayar Akash	978-1-910499-06-1 Hazrat Shahjalal By Mayar Akash	978-1-910499-68-9 The Adventures of Sylheti mazars By Mayar Akash	978-1-910499-21-4 Alphabet Consonants By MAPublisher
978-1-910499-66-5 Yesteryears By Mayar Akash	978-1-910499-07-8 HSJ Urus By Mayar Akash	978-1-910499-38-2 Bite Size Islam: 99 Names of Allah By Mayar Akash	978-1-910499-22-1 Vowels & Short By MAPublisher

ISBN/Titles /Image/Author	ISBN/Titles /Image/Author	ISBN/Titles /Image/Author	ISBN/Titles /Image/Author
978-1-910499-15-3 Anthology One By Penny Authors	978-1-910499-36-8 Delirious By Liam Newton	978-1-910499-52-8 Lit From Within By Ruth Lewarne	978-1-910499-57-3 The Vampire of the Resistance By Ruth Lewarne
978-1-910499-17-7 Anthology Two By Penny Authors	978-1-910499-54-2 Book of Lived v6 Penny Authors	978-1-910499-49-8 Cry for Help By B. M. Gandhi	978-1-910499-55-9 Riversolde By Meriyon
978-1-910499-29-0 Book of Lived v3 By Penny Authors	978-1-910499-37-5 When You Look Back By Rashma Mehta	978-1-910499-14-6 The Halloweeen Poem by Zainab Khan	978-1-910499-70-2 Smiley & The Acorn By Roger Underwood
978-1-910499-351 V4 Book of Lived By Penny Authors	978-1-910499-37-5 My Dream World By Rashma Mehta	978-1-910499-69-6 Consciousness By Mustak Mustafa	978-1-910499-40-5 World's First University By Giasuddin Ahmed
978-1-910499-50-4 Book of Lived v5 By Penny Authors	978-1-910499-53-5 Angel Eyez By Rashma Mehta	978-1-910499-73-3 Book of Lived v7 By Penny Authors	978-1-910499-56-6 The Warrior Queen By Giasuddin Ahmed

www.mapublisher.org.uk

Res Burman's Poetry Volume 2

ISBN/Titles /Image/Author	ISBN/Titles /Image/Author	ISBN/Titles /Image/Author	ISBN/Titles /Image/Author
978-1-910499-58-0 Tower Hamlets, Random, One Mayar Akash	978-1-910499-60-3 Tower Hamlets, Random, Two By Mayar Akash	978-1-910499-05-4 Tide of Change By Mayar Akash	978-1-910499-51-1 Brick & Mortar By Mayar Akash
978-1-910499-61-0 Grenfell Tower By Mayar Akash	978-1-910499-63-4 Power Houses By Mayar Akash	978-1-910499-71-9 Altab Ali Murder By Mayar Akash	978-1-910499-31-3 Pathfinders By Mayar Akash
978-1-910499-62-7 Community Service 1992-1993 By Mayar Akash	978-1-910499-64-1 Bancroft Estate By Mayar Akash	978-1-910499-11-5 Re-Awakening By Mayar Akash	978-1-910499-13-9 Chronicle of Sylhetis of UK By Mayar Akash
978-1-910499-59-7 Brick Lane, Spitalfields By Mayar Akash	978-1-910499-72-6 25th Anniversary of Bangladesh By Mayar Akash	978-1-910499-12-2 Young Voice Mayar Akash	978-1-910499-42-9 Bangladeshi Fishes By Mayar Akash
978-1-910499-65-8 PYO Polish Exchange 1992 By Mayar Akash	978-1-910499-30-6 TH Bangladeshi Politicians By Mayar Akash	978-1-910499-10-8 Vigil Subotaged By Mayar Akash	978-1-910499-67-2 F. Ahmed and History By Mukid Choudhury

www.mapublisher.org.uk

Res J. F. Burman

ISBN/Titles /Image/Author	ISBN/Titles /Image/Author	ISBN/Titles /Image/Author	ISBN/Titles /Image/Author
978-1-910499-43-6 My Life Book 1 By Mayar Akash	978-1-910499-44-3 My Life Book 2 By Mayar Akash	978-1-910499-45-0 My Life Book 3 By Mayar Akash	978-1-910499-46-7 My Life Book 4 By Mayar Akash
978-1-910499-47-4 My Life Book 5 By Mayar Akash	978-1-910499-75-7 Bangladeshis in Manchester - Oral History, Part 1 By M.A. Mustak	978-1-910499-74-0 Peter Fox Artist (LE) A Re-enchantment of Contemporary Art By Peter Fox	978-1-910499-78-8 On The Seventh Day By Cosette Ratliff
978-1-910499-79-5 Altab Ali Life & Family By Mayar Akash	978-1-910499-77-1 Smiley & the Acorn Treasure on the Isles of Scilly By Roger Underwood	978-1-910499-80-1 India – stories from the Banyan Tree Paul Wadsworth	978-1-910499-84-9 V8 Book of lived Penny Authors
978-1-910499-87-0 Behind the tears Rashma Mehta	978-1-910499-85-6 RhythmScripts My Feet is just mine Libby Pentreath	978-1-910499-89-4 Podgy and the Delightful Company John Dillon	978-1-910499-90-0 Calm and the Storm Alison Norton
9781910499924 Res Burman's Poetry V1 Res Burman	9781910499887 Pebble Libby Pentreath	9781910499917 The Crab's Tale John Dillon	9781910499962 Lowry's Boats Roger Lowry

www.mapublisher.org.uk

www.ingramcontent.com/pod-product-compliance
Lightning Source LLC
Chambersburg PA
CBHW050842160426
43192CB00011B/2121